The Question *of* Water

Written by Mary-Anne Creasy

Flying Start
to Literacy®

Contents

Introduction

Water is a precious resource that we cannot live without. It is used by people all around the world every day. People use water for drinking, washing, cleaning and growing food. In fact, water is used to make everything we use every day.

Most of the water that people use comes from rivers and lakes. Clever ways have been developed to store and deliver this water to the people who need it. Once the water has been used, it can be cleaned so it can be used again – we can recycle water.

As the number of people on Earth grows, the demand on our water supply increases. In the future we will need to be even more careful about how we look after and use our precious water supply.

Water fact

In the past 50 years, the world's population has increased by almost four billion people, but the amount of water has stayed the same.

Where does water come from?

The next time you have a drink of water, think about where this water came from.

The water you are drinking may have fallen as rain last week, but it is not new water. It has been around for as long as Earth has been here. Every drop of water on Earth has been here since Earth began.

There will never be any more water on Earth than there is now. This water is always moving and the same water is used over and over again. It moves from the surface of the Earth into the air, and back to the surface again. This is called the water cycle.

The water cycle

All water on Earth is part of the water cycle. This is how the water cycle works:

1. The water in rivers, lakes and oceans gets heated by the sun and turns into a gas called water vapour. The vapour moves up into the air. This is called evaporation.

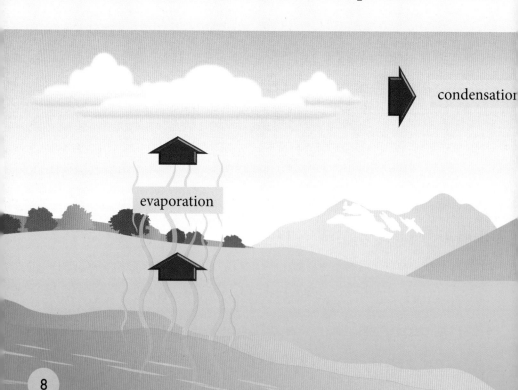

condensation

evaporation

2. In the air the water vapour cools down and turns into water droplets. This is called condensation. You can see these water droplets as they form clouds.

3. When there are a lot of water droplets in the clouds, they become very heavy. The air cannot hold the water anymore and the water falls back to Earth as rain, hail, sleet or snow. This is called precipitation.

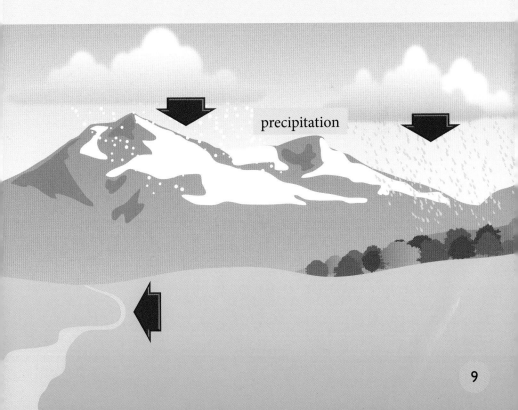

precipitation

Where is all the water?

We need fresh water, but only a tiny amount of all the water on Earth is fresh water. Most of the fresh water on Earth is frozen in glaciers and ice caps in Antarctica and the Arctic. We cannot use it for drinking or to grow crops.

Arctic

Only a tiny portion of the Earth's fresh water is found on the surface of the Earth. This water is in lakes, rivers,

Antarctica

streams, swamps and ponds. Most of the water we use for drinking and for growing crops comes from rivers and lakes.

Some fresh water is found under the ground. It is called groundwater. There is much more fresh water under the ground than on the Earth's surface.

Although Earth is covered in water, most of this water is in the oceans. Ocean water is salt water and we cannot drink it or use it to grow crops.

Water fact

Nearly all the water on Earth is salt water and we cannot use it.

97%

2.4% 0.6%

salt water | frozen water | fresh water

How do we get water?

In most places around the world, people can easily get water by turning on taps in their homes. The water is pumped from the water supply through pipes and into homes. Drinking water is filtered and cleaned before it goes through the pipes.

Water is collected and stored in water tanks.

In some places, people get their water from tanks that collect water when it rains. Other people get their water straight from rivers, dams or lakes close to their homes.

This is a pump station on a lake. It pumps water from the lake for people to use.

The Golden Pipeline

What happens when people don't have a fresh water supply close by?

When gold was discovered in a desert area of Western Australia in 1892, thousands of people travelled there to mine for riches. They soon discovered there was barely any fresh, clean water. Clean water was so expensive that it cost nearly one third of a worker's weekly wage just to buy 4.5 litres.

Hundreds of miners died after they caught diseases from drinking dirty water.

The government decided it must take fresh water to the minefields from water supplies 560 kilometres away near Perth.

A few years later, the government began building a pipeline and it was finished in 1903.

More than 100 years later, the Golden Pipeline in Western Australia now supplies fresh water to 100 000 people in towns, as well as to mining projects and farms in an area two thirds the size of Tasmania.

Where does waste water go?

When we brush our teeth, flush the toilet or use the washing machine, we use water. After we have used this water, it is dirty and becomes waste water. There are different sorts of waste water. Waste water from toilets is called black water. Waste water from other parts of a household is called grey water.

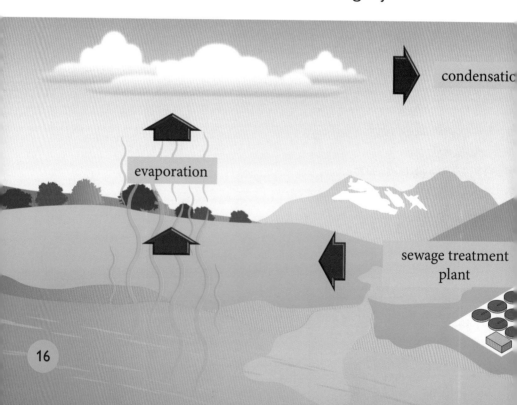

condensatic

evaporation

sewage treatment plant

In most homes, waste water goes down the drain and is taken to a sewage treatment plant. A sewage treatment plant is a huge factory that removes any substances in the water that could harm the environment. When the water is clean, it is returned to a river or lake, or released onto the land. This water becomes a part of the water cycle once again.

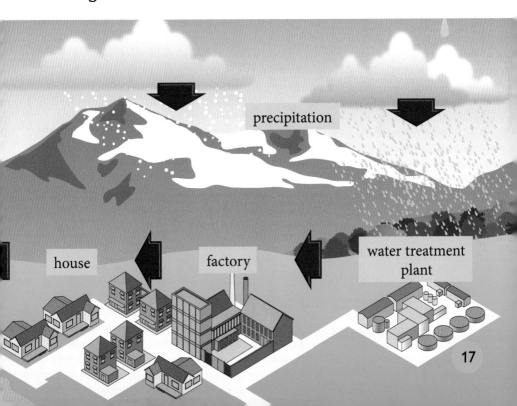

precipitation

house

factory

water treatment plant

How much water is used to make things?

People use water to make or produce almost everything we use.

Nearly three quarters of all fresh water is used by farmers to water their crops. Some crops such as rice and cotton need a lot of water to grow. And water is also used in factories to make the things we use every day.

Water fact

Nearly 11 400 litres of water are used to produce one cotton shirt.

This table shows the average quantities of water used to produce one kilogram of each of four different foods.

Corn: 1000 litres

Wheat: 1500 litres

Rice: 3000 litres

Beef: 16 000 litres*

*This water is used mainly for the production of food for the animal.

 = 500 litres

How much water is used to make a cheeseburger?

When you eat a cheeseburger, you might not think that you are "using water". But did you know that a huge amount of water is used to make one cheeseburger?

The amount of water used to make a cheeseburger is about 2400 litres. Most of this water is used to grow crops for cattle to eat. Cattle eat grass, hay and grains such as oats and barley. All of these crops need water to grow. The cattle are used to make the beef for the hamburger patty.

Water is needed to make the cheese to put on the hamburger. Again, water is needed to feed the cows that produce the milk that is used to make cheese.

Water is also used in factories where the milk is turned into cheese.

Water is used to grow the wheat to make the flour that is used to make the bun. Water is also used to grow other ingredients in the cheeseburger such as tomato and lettuce.

And it takes about 11 litres of water to make one sheet of paper to wrap the cheeseburger!

Is there enough water?

The population of the world is growing. Having more people in the world means that we need more fresh water. Many people are concerned that there may not be enough fresh water for everyone.

In many places people rely on rainfall to fill dams and reservoirs. Due to changing weather patterns there is a lot less rain in some areas and therefore a lot less water can be stored. Some places are running out of water.

Water fact

In some parts of the world people do not have clean, fresh water. They are forced to get their water from rivers and waterholes that are polluted.

Long droughts, a growing population and the pollution of water have made people realise that clean, fresh water is very precious.

But there are many ways to save the fresh water we already have and to use less of it. And there are also ways to create fresh water out of water from the oceans.

The water in this reservoir is getting very low because it has not rained for a long time.

Making fresh water.

Most of the water on Earth is salt water.
In some cities near the ocean, factories have
been built to turn seawater into fresh water.
The process of taking salt out of seawater
to make fresh water is called desalination,
and it can happen in two ways.

The first way is for seawater to be forced
through very tiny filters to remove the salt.

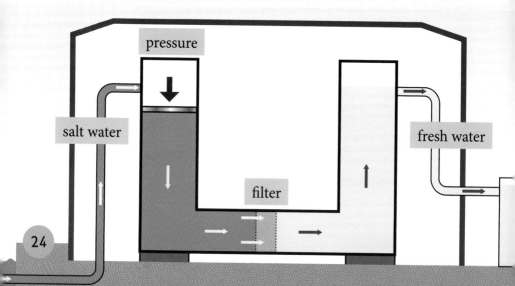

pressure

salt water

fresh water

filter

The second way is to heat seawater in large tanks. When the vapour from the hot seawater cools down, it creates droplets of fresh water on the inside walls of the tanks. This water is then collected.

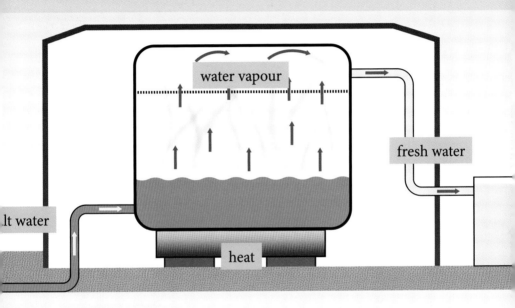

water vapour

fresh water

lt water

heat

Water fact

Sailors used small desalination machines on their sailing boats about 2000 years ago. These machines had filters to remove the salt from seawater.

Can I do anything to help?

There are a lot of things you can do to save water. Every drop of water you save helps the world's water supplies.
Here are some ideas:

- Take shorter showers.
- Check that you have a water-saving shower-head fitted.

- Turn off the tap when you brush your teeth.

Check for dripping taps at home and at school.

Water your garden in the cool parts of the day. This stops the water evaporating before it is used by the plants.

Make sure the washing machine and dishwasher are full before they are turned on.

Encourage other people to save water, too.

A note from the author

The large city where I live suffered a drought for about six years. The water level in our city's dam got so low that we were not allowed to water our gardens or wash our cars. Many people bought rainwater tanks to collect the small amount of rain that did fall. The people in our city became some of the best water savers in the modern world, so I had a personal interest when writing this book.

Many people try to conserve water today. But there is water usage that is hidden in things that we eat and things that we buy. This was the most surprising information I found, and being aware of it may be the next step to becoming better water savers.